The Buses Roll

The Buses Roll

Photographs by

CAROL BALDWIN and PETER T. WHITNEY

Text by ROBERT COLES   Preface by ERIK H. ERIKSON

Edited by LINN UNDERHILL

W.W. Norton & Company, Inc. *New York*

Copyright © 1974 by W. W. Norton & Company, Inc.

First Edition

Library of Congress Cataloging in Publication Data
Baldwin, Carol.
  The buses roll.
  1. School integration—Berkeley, Calif.—Pictorial
works. 2. Berkeley, Calif.—Schools. I. Whitney, Peter, illus. II. Coles, Robert. III.
Title.
LA 245.B4B34   370.19'342   74-11072
ISBN 0-393-05529-9
ISBN 0-393-05535-3 (pbk.)

Published simultaneously in Canada
by George J. McLeod Limited, Toronto

Printed in the United States of America
1 2 3 4 5 6 7 8 9 0

PREFACE

One of the first things I see when I get up in the morning is an enlarged photograph done by Carol Baldwin in Senegal. It shows four slim black children starkly silhouetted against a blindingly white house front. They are initiating a dance. The first and tallest is standing very straight, arms held close to her sides. The second one with a mischievous smile lifts one hand suggestively: there is going to be a happening. The third raises one foot and lifts one hand with fingers spread; and the fourth, finally, lets go: the whole body bends to the beat of a dance rhythm that one knows will spark the others. Such parsimony of motion and of communication could not have been "directed." Yet one has the impression that these children are responding to the special challenge of the photographer's presence, that they are somehow aware of representing something beyond themselves and beyond the moment. This is what we may envy the good photographer: not just the eye that searches and finds people unaware in expressions, postures, and groupings worth preserving for endless review, but also that presence of personality that makes subjects wish to be pictorial witnesses in what otherwise may be an ordinary occurrence.

Carol Baldwin had that presence. And if I have now described a picture taken as far away as Senegal, it is in order to indicate the range of her work, which originated in Berkeley, often went abroad, and at a

6 significant moment focused again on Berkeley, where she found a co-worker in Peter Whitney. I also wanted to underline the essential truth that good photographers are always strangers entering into a scene, even a familiar one, as eyewitnesses of the timeless significance of time-bound events.

The Berkeley busing, however, while enacted by familiar people on familiar territory, was no everyday event: it was the consummation of years of conflict in this more than ordinarily aware community. The pictorial record of the busing itself, of course, does not chronicle the severe struggle these citizens had experienced in the preceding months and years, within their individual consciences as well as in heated debates in homes and on the streets, in small conferences and in mass meetings. Only after much concerted and patient collaboration of school staff and community members had a busing plan been formulated, and at last the question of "How do we do it?" replaced that of "Should we do it?" It was in January 1968 at a meeting attended by over two thousand people that the school board accepted this plan for the desegregation of the elementary schools. The final scene of that crisis, when in the fall of 1968 the buses bravely began to roll, is pictured in this book.

Robert Coles tells some of the story. Although Carol and he did not meet there, we learned by lucky accident that this omnipresent man had been in Berkeley, too, and that, in fact, another eyewitness account was waiting in his files—or shall I call it an earwitness account, which supplemented Carol's and Peter's visual record? For it is clear that Coles, in all his work, is the social doctor who listens, able to engage the wish and ability of those engaged in social change of putting into words such worries and hopes as we may, in fact, assume to have been on the minds of those who, in the scenes depicted by Carol and Peter, staunchly step into their new roles. Coles, furthermore, has done this kind of recording in depth so systematically and on such a wide scale that he is, indeed, just the right man to put the Berkeley busing into the perspective of comparable events all over the nation.

Together, then, the photographers and the doctor are the eye and the ear

of a new way of recording history-in-the-making, which may well be part of a new way of making history. For when our memories are flooded by false hopes or, indeed, false despair, we can always go back to rare books such as this one and find an intimate record of what people really looked like and what they said in their own words when they played their part in significant change.

Carol died in 1972, mourned by a community of "subjects" as well as by her close friends. Come to think of it, what other art form permits the artist to leave behind a pictorial record as a wordless memorial? For it preserves a dialogue not only between a medium and the world of appearances but also between the artist's presence and his human subjects, who, caught in their response to the occasion, often seem not merely reflected in the encounter but obviously enriched by it.

ERIK H. ERIKSON

This book is dedicated to the children of Berkeley, Calif.

THE BEGINNING... The Buses Roll

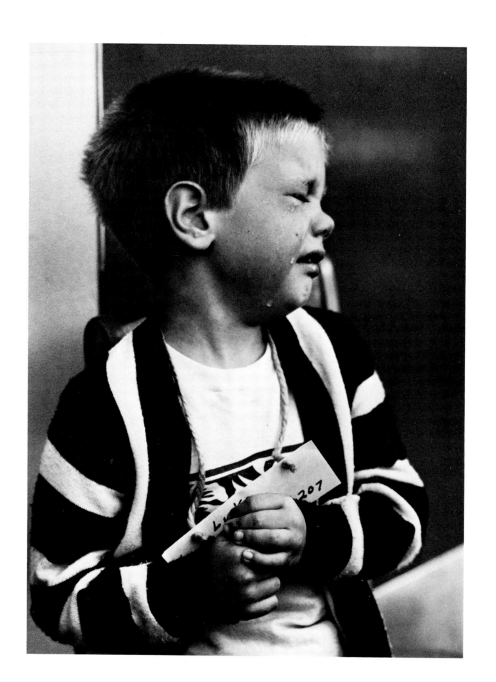

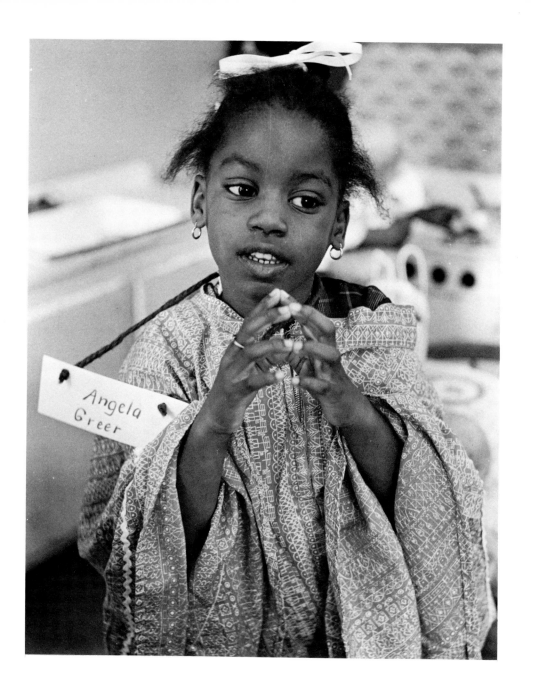

The pictures in this book tell a story which now is, **23** ironically, more familiar to Southerners than Californians or the rest of us who live in the West or the North's crowded and, for the most part, racially segregated cities. For years federal courts have insisted that black children once by law kept apart be sent to previously all-white schools. Usually such orders have required busing, and the result, in cities like Memphis or Charlotte, North Carolina, has been a substantial amount of travel for white children as well as black ones—though one has to add that for a long time throughout the region white children have traveled on buses, passing one, maybe two black schools on their way to their own school, even as black children have done the same. If such *de jure* segregation is increasingly, even in the rural counties of Mississippi or Alabama, a thing of the past, then *de facto* segregation is, one begins to think at times, the wave of the future.

I remember, for instance, Atlanta. I lived and worked there for two years, starting in 1961, when ten black youths entered four white high schools, amid a good deal of fear on the part of everyone in the city— New Orleans having the year before gone through mobs and violence when four black children, each age six, had entered two white elementary schools. I had witnessed that violence, and heard it talked about when the ten Atlanta black families came together, before the opening of school. Still, the young men and women were determined, and the rest is history: a relatively peaceful entry, followed by a quiet school year, in turn followed by an increase the next year in the numbers of black children going to white schools. By 1963 Atlanta seemed to offer the entire nation hope: black children, both poor and middle class, were riding buses to white schools in a deeply southern state, and upon arrival were being treated, as I kept on hearing, "just like anyone else." Yet today two of the four all-white high schools initially integrated in 1961 are all black, the white school population of the city drops year by year, even as the number of blacks in schools rises, and Atlanta is well on its way to being a northern city, with residential areas demarcated firmly by race, and with a virtually all-white suburban noose around the city.

Last year, on the occasion of an annual visit I make to the city, a now grown and married black woman, who over ten years ago rode to a white school on a bus—she was the only black on it—made this observation to me: "I wonder, sometimes, what the point of it all was. I'd get on that bus and I'd remember my mother's words: 'You're going there for all of us. Keep your chin up.' I kept my chin up, and I tried to ignore the insults, and after a while they stopped coming. I was left alone, strictly alone! That wasn't pleasant, either. But I did all right; I know I did all right. The last day, when I got off the bus, the bus driver said to me, 'You've done a good job, and your people should be proud of you.' And he was so mean to me at the beginning, always telling me I should sit in one place or another, so that there would be 'peace and quiet' on the bus, and giving me those looks of his. I once dreamed he drove that bus of his into the side of a brick building, and it was all smashed up, and I was the only one to walk away alive. But that was a long time ago, and since then we've had more and more desegregation—and look what it's meant: the same old all-black schools and all-white schools. They'll soon be driving black children a hundred miles a day, if they're going to go to white

schools; and like my mother says, they'll still be running from us. So there's
no use trying to be with them, because a scared person is not good company.
That's why I don't want any more busing; no more of it, until the whites try
chasing us!"

So it goes in the "progressive" South. It is the "deep," rural South which
still experiences integration, sometimes with astonishing success. In those
out-of-the-way towns and villages, where, in contrast to what obtains in
cities, black and white families have known one another intimately, for all
the inequality and worse that prevailed, school buses pick up children of both
races and take them to *the* school, or maybe one of two or three. There are
tensions; and ominously, in a number of counties in states like Mississippi,
Alabama, and Louisiana, private schools or "academies" have appeared, often
under the sponsorship of churches, as a means of enabling white children to
learn by themselves. But so far the Deep South seems almost nostalgically
taken up with the integration struggle that began in the late 1950s for the upper
South and the larger cities of the lower South. And so far, as I keep hearing
from school officials in the Mississippi Delta or in south-central Alabama,
the North or West furnish no example of leadership with respect to integration. "What are they doing up there?" I hear that again and again, and one
searches for answers, however insubstantial: a busing program in Boston or
Minneapolis, Syracuse or Hartford. And such programs are not to be lightly
dismissed, because in those cities and others, too, serious efforts have been
made to bring white and black children together in schools, in the hope that
each "group" will learn a good deal about and from the other.

Nevertheless, as I went about the country, in 1968 and 1969, trying to gain
a sense of what was and what was not working, so far as school desegregation
went, outside the South, I found relatively few cities which were really com-

26 mitted thoroughly to a joint effort, on the part of black and white people, to the shared education of their children. Usually the desegregation programs came about this way: rising dissatisfaction on the part of a segment of the black community with the education black children have been receiving; protests by a relative handful of blacks, occasionally joined by veteran white civil rights activists, often from suburbs unlikely to be affected by the struggle under way; resistance on the part of a diffuse, unorganized white community, which, however, slowly becomes alarmed, angered, and all too responsive to the opportunistic manipulations of politicians, who (it has to be added) gain strength because their constituents feel themselves threatened and made vulnerable and, very important, put at the mercy of various high-sounding "outsiders" (again from distant suburbs) who speak noble sentiments, but manage to keep their own children far away from the conflict, while all the while looking down upon "them," the "racists"; next, a confrontation or, more likely, a series of confrontations, on the streets, in the courts, at the polls, all covered widely by reporters and television cameras; and, finally, a program of sorts, involving a rearrangement of school districts and the use of buses to shift percentages at least somewhat toward racially "balanced" schools.

Who rides those buses? Commonly it has been black children, and at first their parents were only too willing, as I well know from my work with black families in Boston during the middle and late 1960s. For one school year I rode on a bus myself with black children, and saw the hope, the yearning, the expectation the parents of those children felt and communicated to their sons and daughters: "I try to tell my daughter every morning, while she is eating her breakfast, that when she gets on that bus, she's building a future for herself, and when she enters that school, she's doing some more building, and when she leaves the school in the afternoon, she's put in a day of building, besides learning her numbers and her letters." The child got the message. Often she seemed too serious, too intent on doing that "building" her mother kept

on mentioning. Once she even drew a picture for me, a way she could let me know how obedient, attentive, and patient she was: a tower of brick, from which she could see all of Boston. Below were some houses she declared to be her own and those of her neighbors. I suppose a sociologist might in connection with the subject matter refer to "upward social mobility."

Meanwhile, on the other side of town white families were by no means friendly when the bus entered their neighborhood. They had not been consulted. And when they spoke up, they were fought, then defeated. Here is how one white woman, speaking about a busing program in Boston but sounding like many others who live elsewhere, North and South, East and West, tried to put across her complicated range of feelings: "I'm not against any individual child. I am *not* a racist, no matter what those high-and-mighty suburban liberals with their picket signs say. I just won't have my children bused to some god-awful slum school, and I don't want children from God knows where coming over here. We put our last cent into this home. We both work to keep up with the mortgage and all the expenses. We're not rich; we can't afford to be generous at someone else's expense. We just want to live peacefully out here. We want our children to grow up in a quiet, decent neighborhood. We want to be able to go out of our house without carrying a gun or holding on to a German police dog. We want to see them off to school, and not sit for the rest of the day wondering, Are they safe, and will there be a big fight, and are they afraid even to walk home if they miss the bus? That's why I'm opposed to bringing kids from one kind of section into another; it's going against what's natural for both groups of people. And if they try to take *our* children across the city, just because some college professors and professional agitators and all the rest say they should go, then, like my husband said, we'll have a civil war right up here in the North! Anyway, no one asks us about anything, so I guess we're going to have to learn how to band together and take care of ourselves."

For her and people like her all over the country school desegregation entails not only social and economic threats but a kind of political affront: others flex their muscles and begin to make their point, whereas "ordinary, working people," the way she describes her husband and herself and their neighbors, "have to sit back," as she puts it, "and take it, always take it." Taking it, she registers surprise, annoyance, resentment, confusion, fear, anger—and, not least, a sense of powerlessness, conveyed sometimes in the briefest but most plaintive of questions: "Why us?" And, for a while, many of us involved in one way or another with the civil rights movement had little interest in answering such a question. She was a "racist" or a "covert racist"—that is, if we even thought about her at all. Chances were we didn't, at least in the beginning, call people like her anything at all. There were, in our minds, the blacks, a terribly hurt and denied people, and us, their allies. The point was to fight against segregationists in the South—visible, palpable, all too sturdy and adroit opponents, not without the power that a small but shrewd and inventive band of United States Senators can mobilize; and as for the North, there were measures to be taken, initiatives to be undertaken, if necessary, and causes to fight and win through legislation. Who had time or, alas, the inclination to stop and think about how a white housewife in a so-called "streetcar suburb" (a modest, lower-middle-class neighborhood, not all that far from what we have come to think of as the "inner city") feels about the social changes taking place in this country? Are not blacks victims, whites the fortunate ones, if not the oppressors? Is it not a clear-cut matter of right and wrong? Were there not centuries of injustice to atone for, work against, begin to set right?

Those are rhetorical questions, yet they can all too easily be mobilized against those who, for their own reasons, say, "No, keep things as they were," or "Send them elsewhere," a virtual refrain for anyone who wants to hear the "attitudes" expressed in the white neighborhoods of various American cities. In 1968 and 1969 I went to thirteen of those northern and western cities, in hopes of gaining some sense of what was happening in various attempts at school desegregation. I have written up (in the third volume of *Children of Crisis: The South Goes North*) what I saw and heard, and one city's experience described was that of West Park, a thinly disguised pseudonym for Berkeley, which I visited for over a week in the autumn of 1968, just as an extraordinary attempt to bring white and black children together was getting under way. I was enormously moved and impressed. I was also made curious: how did this particular community manage to do such a fine job?

Rather obviously, Berkeley is in several respects unusual: it is a university city, and a city that is not so large that its university population is virtually without significance numerically. There is a substantial black population—and an absence of the large-scale industry a city like Detroit possesses. That is to say, the city's black population tends to be more "established" than is the case in the large industrial cities of the East or, for that matter, Los Angeles. Berkeley also has a large upper-middle-class constituency, apart from its university population. (Not that wealth is by any means associated with a willingness to yield power and welcome others as brothers—and fit companions for one's children.) Such a constituency is made up of those who may be in business or the professions, as opposed to university employees, but want to have some involvement, however occasional or tangential to a campus—in this case one rather well known as, at the very least, "liberal" or "progressive." Still, the city of Berkeley is not to be confused with the campus of the University of California at Berkeley, something that ought to be carefully held in mind. If things went exceedingly well, by and large, for the children (and teachers) shown in this book's photographs, the explanation cannot be the one I heard all too many Easterners give when I went home and sang the praises of Berkeley's schools: "Oh, of course—a big university town."

Berkeley is that, but it is also a city where one can meet "plain, ordinary working people," even "ex-Southerners." Those were two self-descriptions I heard while there, and what followed had the ring of the familiar for me; in both the South and the North I had heard the sincerely and emotionally stated complaints: "It's the usual combination—the university people and the Negroes. I'm not against Negro people; I work with them, and I like them. I wouldn't mind them living right next door to me, if only they were good people, clean and law-abiding. What I object to—it's hard to say. Mostly, it's the idea of sending children away from their neighborhood schools. They'd have to go to a school I don't believe I've ever seen. Why should we do that? It's an insult to the Negroes as much as us. Do they need white people in order to learn? Do my children have to be bused clear across the city just so they can have a few more Negroes in their classrooms? What difference does it make?"

Yet, the speaker did not sustain that attitude. She attended a community meeting, one of many held in Berkeley before school desegregation began, and she heard her own sentiments voiced by others. She also heard arguments made against her point of view. She was not immediately converted; in fact, I doubt if she would ever describe herself as in favor of the city's plan to integrate each and every one of its schools. But she at least felt that her grievances were heard and, very important, she knew that families like hers were not being asked to shoulder the entire burden of a difficult social and educational crisis, while others, far better off economically and far more influential in the city, expressed dismay at "racists" or "bigots" and enormous sympathy for "the poor" or "the blacks"—while protected in every way from personal involvement through their children in the program. Nor is it merely a matter

of misery liking company. True, one resents moralistic self-righteousness
from any quarter, and especially when it comes from those who get not a
finger wet, not a toe stubbed, but simply sit back as wordy onlookers. But the
fears many working-class people have about school integration have their
own sources—and are not simply thinly disguised grudges tied to class con-
sciousness: us as against the rich, with their new-found objects of compassion,
the blacks.

"We moved here from Oakland. A cousin of mine said I should have
stayed in Oakland, so it won't become all black. She's our rich cousin; her
husband is a doctor, and *they* live in Marin County. Advice comes easy when
it's not your own family at stake, and when you can have a nice, comfortable
life, with maybe a few very refined Negro neighbors in the same town. I want
to make this point: my husband is an accountant, and he hasn't any prejudices, and we're not 'nervous, insecure people.' That's what I read in one of
those college publications—that there are 'nervous, insecure people' who are
opposed to the new busing program. We tried to stay in Oakland. I didn't
want to move. I hate moving; once I'm settled in a place, I want to stay there
for life. I had real close friends, Negro neighbors. *They* want to move from
Oakland, too. Is it so hard for people to realize that it isn't necessarily racial
prejudice that makes me wonder about all this busing—about my children
going far from here to a school in a neighborhood that is not theirs, and with
children who don't live near them? I know all the arguments: in a democracy
we should all get the same break, and try to know each other. I'm in favor of
that. But I don't see why young children should bear the brunt of social
change, especially when a lot of the people who are pushing this kind of
experiment don't have a thing to risk themselves.

"Let me tell you what I think: I think the problem is that there are poor
people, uneducated people, who have come here from the South, and their

34   Instead, all too often, social scientists or psychiatrists go after, so to speak, such a person: what does she think about X, what would she do in the event of Y, how does she handle Z alternative when it is mentioned to her? Not that we don't learn something important from that line of inquiry: questionnaires, standardized tests, or, in my own case, a series of questions based upon certain interests the observer has and wants to get stated, explored, documented. (Even if there were substantial objections—invasion of privacy, absurdity of the questions, an affront to the intelligence or dignity of those "interrogated" —one doubts if these days much can be done: polls and surveys and research projects are part of modern American life.) But I fear that all too often a caricature of a person, and even a distortion of his or her thinking, comes across in those "results" or "write-ups" that are now given so much authority. The woman I have just quoted is indeed "nervous" and "insecure"; but so are others, including those who welcome integration, welcome busing. Nervous about what? Insecure in connection with which ideas or proposals? Maybe some upper-middle-class, avowedly "liberal" parents also have moments of nervousness or insecurity. Maybe their views, like those of the accountant's wife, have a touch of the automatic, the reflexive: I had better take this stand or position on that issue or question, because that is what everyone else I associate with, or want to associate with, will say or affirm.

In any event, all over this nation the experience Berkeley had is not to be taken for granted. In that particular city a thorough effort was made at integration, rather than desegregation; and, from what I saw, the effort was remarkably successful. The issue was not only numbers, though that is an important matter, because a handful of black (or white) children in the midst of a whole school of white (or black) children makes for constant apprehension, as a number of southern black children who pioneered school desegregation in the 1960s can testify. But beyond a "balance" of black and white children, there is the matter of what happens to those children during those hours at school. In a sense, the Berkeley schools were not only integrated racially; there was class integration, through and through. Whites from the hills (well-to-do) sent their children, often enough, as far on buses as blacks "down" in the city's poorer districts. And when those children arrived at their schools, they were greeted by teachers and assistant principals and principals who very much wanted to *begin* with the new situation before them, rather than consider it an end in itself—so-and-so percentages of black and white children. So weeks before and weeks after those buses began to roll, there were all kinds of meetings, discussions, efforts to stop and consider what it was, in the way of values and assumptions, that a new policy was bringing together—it being one thing to bring together those values and assumptions and quite another to enable the children who hold them to share, to teach one another, and thereby to learn. And maybe unlearn a few things, too.

Nor was it—is it ever?—purely a matter of white fearfulness or narrowness or patronizing "helpfulness." Blacks have their own worries and blind spots and legacy of "defensiveness" in the face of fear or anxiety—their particular kind of "nervousness" or "insecurity." Blacks can misread people, or suit themselves with social or psychological interpretations which, in the end, amount to a distorted or even flagrantly wrong vision. And blacks, too, can be poignantly open and honest: "I worry about all this. I worry for my own people. I worry about the white people of this city. Everyone thinks that Berkeley can't go wrong in this project: we're so liberal and progressive. Well, they're right, in a way. I'm from Chicago, originally. I trained to be a nurse there, and came out here during the Korean war with my husband. He was being sent over, and I went as far as I could with him. But I loved San Francisco, and so did he. We decided we'd live here when he got out, and we did. It was for us almost like the move my parents made out of the South. We felt the breath of fresh air: the Pacific, and the better racial atmosphere. There are so many different groups here. In Chicago it was that one polarization: Negroes and whites. Here there are Chinese and Japanese and Filipinos and Puerto Ricans and Mexican Americans—very cosmopolitan.

"And there's the university, of course. We moved to Berkeley because we wanted to live a quiet and pleasant life and be near the university. My husband is a teacher, and he likes to audit courses, when he can, or go to lectures. Even though he's in favor of this change, we both are worried. We worry about the Negro children: is it too much for them, to be at school with boys and girls who have had so much more, who are far better prepared? I know how I feel with white people, even today. I smile and I know how to be polite and *appear* cool and collected. But there's a part of me that's always watching, always testing. The other day in the hospital a patient asked me what I thought of the Berkeley schools—their 'plan,' he called it, to 'mix up the whole system.' I asked him what he meant: that expression 'mix up' put me on my guard. I found myself staring at him with a hard look. I could feel the tension in my hands. They get tight: the muscles. I end up clasping them at moments like that. I have a friend, a psychiatric nurse, who told me once, when I told her about my reaction, that the reason I do so is I'm angry, and I'm afraid I might hit someone, slap his face. Well, I didn't want to slap that patient's face. I just wanted to cut short our conversation and get out of that room.

"But I had him all wrong. He was being a little playful with me, and I was too suspicious to let him get away with it. He turned out to be a newspaperman, and he told me what he'd seen in Little Rock, when they had all the trouble there. He told me he worried about the white children and I told him I worried about the Negro children. I didn't tell him, but I told myself, Why shouldn't your daughter misinterpret people, the way you just did? Sometimes I think that the worst thing about racial prejudice is what it does to you when you're not even facing it. I can bear a bigot; I can take his talk. It's when I misjudge someone who isn't a bigot at all—when I lose my sense of humor and my judgment about people—that I feel really the victim of 'oppression,' as the students at Berkeley put it. But the students become victims, too; when they keep on trying to tell my husband and me how 'oppressed' we are—how 'deracinated,' one of them said in a lecture—then I say to myself, It's as bad for those lecturers as it is for me; they've lost all perspective, and are as obsessed with race as the people in the Klan. I don't say they're the same as the Klan people. They're on our side, I know. It just bothers me when I get *harangued*.

"And I worry that my children will become as overconscious as I am: What does that white teacher mean, asking me to do that? Why did the white girl say what she did to me? Oh, I've spent a lifetime with those questions. I wish—I hope and pray—that this new busing program will help Negro children, *this* generation of Negro children, to grow up differently. I told my husband the other night that it would be a miracle if the Berkeley schools helped our son and our daughters forget themselves a little. We're beginning to hear more and more about racial pride; well, I'm in favor of it, but I'd like my children to react like human beings first, and Negroes second. I mean, if one child (who happens to be white) comes toward them and smiles, I hope they'll respond to her smile, not think, What does this white chick want, and why is she turning that smile on me? Yes, you have to watch your step in this world. But you can be so watchful about some things you miss a million important other things."

No social observer or interviewer will ever be able to add up any fixed score: Berkeley's effort to integrate its schools was successful by the following percentage. We are prone at this time to look at "hard data": let's have the reading *scores*, the numerical evidence that arithmetic was done better by more children. Without in any way denying the need for those objective measurements, I would again ask that the nuances and subtleties of psychological growth also be taken into consideration. No score on a reading or mathematics test will amount to much if a child feels alone, worthless, looked down upon, or, for that matter, singled out by being elevated to high heaven: that beautiful, beautiful black child!

The nurse just called upon went into her own struggle to affirm herself at far greater length than I can draw upon here; in essence she told me how well she did in Chicago's schools, but how poorly they had served her: "I was taught there; I got an education there. The only thing was I was taught to feel that there wasn't much point to studying, not for me. It so happens that my father was a minister, and he pushed me hard. So I learned in spite of the teachers; that's how I'd put it. But not every Negro child has a father like mine. So the way teachers approach children can make all the difference. And, of course, teachers can do all kinds of things in a classroom. They can pretend to teach, and really give you the impression that you're stupid as can be, and it's a waste of time for you to be in school. They feel they're wasting their time—just collecting their salary—and they let the children know how they feel. You can get things across without saying them out loud."

One way Berkeley prepared for integration was very much in the spirit of that observation; teachers were called together again and again, not to be given rules or regulations, not to be exhorted or told to whistle in the dark: everything will be fine. Rather, they were asked to think carefully about what was going to happen, and why. I was asked to talk with the city's teachers, and saw for myself how conscientiously and sensibly they had prepared

themselves for what would then rather soon face them. They were aware
that the buses and their activity, with a consequent shift in ratio of black/
white students, were but a beginning; over the weeks and months the real
test of success would be those less dramatic and less public moments: a child's
changed sense of himself or of others, as it is acquired ever so gradually. Not
that some teachers (and parents and public officials) didn't want a "method,"
a "technique"—something which could be rather quickly "applied," something
which would once and for all "solve" the "problem." I was asked rather in-
sistently about "groups": would not "sensitivity training" enable teachers to
see their prejudices, and be less at their mercy? I was and am skeptical: with
those groups, all too often, go so much self-consciousness, and often the dan-
ger of endless, rancorous or self-lacerating assaults. Anyway, some teachers
for their own reasons had gone through "group experience," and by no
means were they universally satisfied: "My best friend says she profited
enormously; she found out what a racist she is underneath. And other things,
too! But she says she can't *talk* about what happened; you either experience
it or you don't. For her, now, the world is divided between those who have
had 'group experience' and those who haven't. It's a new kind of 'elect' and
'damned.' And there's a smugness to the talk I hear from her: I know, and
others don't.

"I tried a group; I was a 'tough nut to crack,' they said. I was told I was
condescending to Negroes; that was my 'basic attitude,' and of course it's
'unconscious.' Maybe so. I don't think I have anything against the Negro
children I teach. If anything, I bend over backwards to try to understand their
problems. But that only proves I'm still prejudiced underneath. After a while
I got sick of hearing all that talk. Two or three people ran the show, and it
was name-calling, that's what it came to. Everyone was calling everyone else
names, and if you so much as took a deep breath or scratched yourself, there

was an interpretation. Such stupidity! I thought to myself it would be better if they all went to a football game—or maybe church. This way they were persecuting the few of us who had our reservations. We were the enemy. Until we threw in the towel and became true believers, members in good standing of the 'group,' then we were 'disturbed' or 'troubled.' Talk about self-righteousness! Talk about prejudice! I was a Negro to some of those people!"

That particular teacher, one of seven I spent several days talking with, was a fine teacher: sensitive, thoughtful, hard-working, and dedicated. She needed no "group experience" or "individual therapy" to overcome anything. She had a natural way with children—her way, and maybe no one else's. She was quite firm with children, *all* children. I suppose someone who wanted to rip out of context various words or deeds might call her a somewhat unyielding person, determined to have her way. She tolerated no nonsense—not from white children and not from black children. She spoke up loud and clear, and occasionally was not shy with her hands. She would walk up and pat a child, or hold her hand on his or her shoulder while she said, in effect, yes or no. She was averse to sweet, sentimental, or ingratiating talk: "I see a child doing wrong, and I speak right up. Some teachers have told me that I'd better watch my step, with this new program: the Negro children will 'misunderstand' me, and they'll go home and tell their parents, and I'll soon be down there in the superintendent's office and told to shape up or ship out. Well, if that happens, I'll leave on my own. I'm not going to become a bundle of reflexes—'the teacher of an integrated class,' as defined by so-and-so or some 'team' of educational psychologists.

"If this new program is going to work, it will be because each teacher, in his or her own way, learns enough *from* the children, and offers enough *to* the children. I can't stand all those do's and don'ts. A lot of the time, you instinctively know them, what to do and what not to do. But when I start *thinking*

about rules too much, I become inhibited. I don't any longer respond to the
kids, only to what I've learned I should or shouldn't be saying or doing. That
is a refined way of ignoring children, and destroys one of the most important
things you have to offer: yourself, as a *person*, who is the teacher *you* happen
to be, not some mannequin, spouting clichés—like 'Let us all be brothers
under the skin,' and 'Let us all smile and be good neighbors.'"

She apologizes for her brusqueness. She may have overstated her case, she
admits. There *are* helpful suggestions—rules, more or less, obtained from the
hard experience of many individuals. She has learned a lot in "workshops," even
though at times she scoffs at them: endless statements of the obvious. More-
over, without arrogance, only with an unaffected kind of pride in herself, she
distinguishes herself from certain other teachers she knows: "A school system
is a large operation; there are hundreds and hundreds of people who work in
Berkeley's schools, and what helps some is of no use to others, and vice versa.
I happen to be the kind of person who works best when left alone. When the
principal comes into my classroom, I fall apart. He knows it, too. My closest
friend is the opposite; send an observer to her classroom, and she perks up,
and becomes better than ever. She told me she'd love to have Negro parents
come and watch her, when the new busing program begins. I said no; I don't
want *any* parents, Negro or white, standing around while I teach. I have my
own way of talking with kids. I can't analyze what I do; I just do it. But when
others are around, taking notes on what I do, I freeze. Someone getting a degree in education spent a few days with me once, and she said I was 'intuitive.'
I said I didn't care what I was called, just so long as my children did a good
job learning each year. That's why I dread this new integration plan. Too many
people will be coming through. We'll be like fish in glass bowls. That's not a
good atmosphere for learning. I'll bet there will be at least a hundred Ph.D.

42 theses at the university as a result of this new integration program. They must be sharpening their knives up in sociology and educational psychology; the army of graduate students, and their supervisors, will begin marching any day now."

I suppose I was a member of that "army." I went from school to school, and tried to find out what Berkeley hoped to accomplish and did accomplish. I came up with no momentous "conclusions," simply a sense that for many black and white children, and for their teachers, and for many hundreds of parents, too, an educational decision (which was at the same time a major social and political decision on the part of an American city) had meant rather a lot: new hopes and expectations and, just as well, new sources of apprehension and fear. Only the day-to-day experience that all of those men, women, and children went through would prove "corrective": unreasonable assumptions (if not fantasies) realized for what they were, and by the same token, a host of anxieties shown to be, in the end, unnecessary. Not that a large-scale change like that one goes through without incident. There were no public incidents, only those nods, grimaces, stares which even teachers sometimes miss. Anyway the city had for months, years even, worked itself toward the decision to integrate its schools racially and by class. By the time the schools actually did go through the experience— a shift in school population, and an all-out effort to take advantage of the shift educationally—there was among many a feeling of anticlimax, as well as, of course, a sense of participation in a dramatic and important moment. I spent time with the school system's administrators, from superintendent down, and found among several of them a sense that the most important part of the process they helped make a reality had, in fact, taken place before the much heralded day of onset, when children boarded buses, and newspapers and television cameras paid attention.

As a matter of fact, the way those administrators went about their prepara-
tions, long months of them, had a very important bearing on what happened
later. Here is what one of them felt it important that I keep in mind: "We knew
what *we* wanted; we pictured nicely integrated classrooms in every school
in the city; and we also pictured an atmosphere of trust in each of those classrooms. But even in a city like Berkeley, where you can take for granted a strong
liberal constituency, dedicated to racial cooperation, there are bound to be
problems. For one thing, it's relatively easy for educated, middle-class people
to say that they 'favor integration.' We sent a lot of young people to the South
in 1964 and 1965. They went for a summer and came home, and their parents
were proud of them. (The parents were also scared stiff, but they held on, and
knew that in a couple of months it would be over.) I don't mean to slight the
dedication or sacrifice of those young people. It's just that I believe a family
will find it easier to send a college student off to Mississippi for a month or two
than a six- or seven-year-old child on a bus to a school out of the neighborhood. So we couldn't take anything for granted, not even among people we
knew supported us all the way, at least by virtue of their ideals.

"I'm getting a little philosophical here; but I think you have to do so. It's
only human for people to hold on to the good, quiet, privileged life they've
always known. And it's not our business to go taking things away from people:
tell them, You've got it good, and others have it bad, so let's even things out.
If you go before a community with that idea in mind, and they get the message,
you're going to have a lot of trouble. And my hunch is you'll lose every time,
even in a city like Berkeley. There are about twenty million Negroes in this
country; and about a hundred million white people, at least, must feel way
better off than those Negroes. If you give them the message that the schools
are an instrument of social and economic leveling, you're going to lose a lot
of support, and maybe stir up God knows what reaction. We've already got

44   "The Negro and Mexican American people want 'better schools'—so that their children will live a 'better life,' meaning get jobs, make money, have a slice of the American pie, which others get big, fat helpings of all the time. There are well-to-do people who say, This is a fine idea; and they do so because they want their children to 'meet as many people as possible, from as many backgrounds as possible.' I've heard them use words like that over and over again. They want more for *their* children, too; a 'richer cultural experience.' Then there are those who say no; they are blunt, and admit that they are afraid they're some: 'white backlash' they call it. By the 1970s there may be a lot more of it. That's why I think we have to be very careful—not cautious or compromising, but careful to spell out exactly why we think all this reorganization, this busing and rearrangement of pupil assignments, makes *educational* sense. We have to say what we believe should happen—and why. We have to show what might happen, given changes. We have to be honest, give a rationale which we believe, and do it in a way others can understand.

    "I worry about myself sometimes. I know what I want: better schooling for children who desperately need it (Negro and Mexican American children) and a broader kind of education for children from the middle-class world, who sometimes grow up with blinders on, not knowing how others think or feel or live, or what they have to learn to accept for themselves. But I wonder whether the people of Berkeley really understand what we are trying to do. I may sound arrogant now: *I* know, but 'they' don't! I don't mean to sound like that. I just worry that we're going into something that will require a lot of energy and dedication, and it will only *begin* when the schools have shifted into the new pupil assignments. And for various groups the reasons to justify the program may be quite different—to the point that even if I *did* get my message across, I might be laughed at, or maybe looked at as a naïve guy, well-intentioned but not much more.

going to lose something: they've struggled and got hold of a little, and now others are going to take it from them — on the one hand the Negroes with their demands, and on the other hand the rich and upper-middle-class people with their generosity, which a workingman may feel is being extended at someone else's expense, because those with a lot of money can afford to be more generous than those with a house and a quarter acre or less, all with a mortgage, and no big pile of stocks and all the rest.

"Well, my job is to tell all these people that apart from their ambitions and their real differences of position in our society, there's a very good reason to make this program work: all of their children, all of the city's children, will learn more. And I don't mean learn more about other 'cultures' or 'groups,' though I know that will happen, and is important. I believe these children will provide ferment for each other, and they *all* will do better in the end. There is evidence to support the view, so academic good sense coincides with the spirit of our Founding Fathers. And speaking of them, their genius was to respond to local movements, all the town meetings and the community uprisings. I hope we have shown here in Berkeley that even in this century (when so much of our life is impersonal, when the cities are so big and crowded, and when people know few families nearby, never mind across the city) we can have a reasonable degree of community agreement on a very important issue."

I have edited several long conversations, but I have kept out much that was eloquent, as well as leaving in remarks that I do feel are among the most impressive I have heard in the years I have spent listening to people. There is no easy summary for what happened in Berkeley. The photographs in this book show the essence of it: uncertainty; tentativeness; the reaching out that children demonstrate, whatever their hesitations; a beginning of friendliness and trust. The result is no City on the Hill; Berkeley today, over five years later, has its fair share of tension and even rancor. The people who used the word "Negro" now refer to "blacks"; and those blacks, like others elsewhere, continue to press for various rights and for a larger share of this nation's wealth. That is to say, integrated schools have not made for the kind of larger harmony some of these photographs might incline the reader to think of as just about realized.

"Wait until those children get older!" I heard from many people in 1968. The implication was that a blissful future had been secured. Alas, when those children do (did) get older they learn (have learned) what we all either know or work hard psychologically not to know—that what is learned in school, objectively (facts) or subjectively (about people, about ourselves), is only a beginning. The point, of course, is to make do—to have work, to get a decent wage, to be treated by others (on the street, in stores, as a citizen, a consumer, a neighbor) with proper and continuing respect. The point is to find in the "grown-up" world, after all those lessons, after all the teachers heard and all the notebooks filled and questions answered and papers written and received back corrected, some recognition of one's worth—as a member of a community, as a human being, as a citizen of a nation, as a creature of God's. If Berkeley's effort managed rather well to bring its various children together in a thoughtful and thoroughly American way ("We hold these truths to be self-evident: that all men are created equal;...endowed by their Creator with certain unalienable rights;...life, liberty, and the pursuit of happiness") then the real test for those children (and for America) will come in the 1970s and 1980s, as those children do indeed become adults, husbands and wives, and then parents.

Will a substantial amount of fine, sensitive schooling be the prelude to a more decent and honorable life? Will the lessons learned in the classroom be repeated later on: more lessons learned about one's essential value as a person? And, very important as an absolutely necessary proof of that value, will one find work and keep work and be rewarded enough for so doing—to the point that there is sufficient food and clothing and shelter for the family to which one belongs? Or will splendid early lessons later be seen as illusions? All those nice words, nice gestures, nice times—they soon enough have turned into the daily nightmare of the ghetto. As for the well-to-do, their children can also find themselves cheated when they grow up. All those pleasant moments, all the attempts, not always easily made, to know strangers—all in vain. Instead there are the strife, bitterness, and fear which a racially divided or socially unstable (and unjust) society generates. So the pictures a gifted photographer took are a moment of history captured and given us. We look. We are helped to see. We learn from them; we are helped to think. Perhaps most of all, we wonder, What will happen to those children later on? Put differently, What will happen to us as a nation? No book of photographs, no written history, either, can ever supply us with the answers to questions like those. We are living out the answers, each of us, each town or city right now. We have been fortunate to have had among us the schoolchildren, schoolteachers, and school officials of Berkeley, all of whom have been engaged in their particular search for those answers. One can only hope their example will prove contagious—a lesson of sorts for others of us to learn.

"If this new program is going to work,
it will be because each teacher, in his or her
own way, learns enough from the children,
and offers enough to the children."

2x0=0
2x1=2
2x2=4
3x0=0
3x1=3
3x2=6
3x3=9
3x4=12
3x5=15
3x6=18
3x7=21
3x8=24
3x9=27
4x0=0
4x1=4
4x2=8
4x3=12
4x4=16
4x5=20
4x6=24
4x7=28
Venita

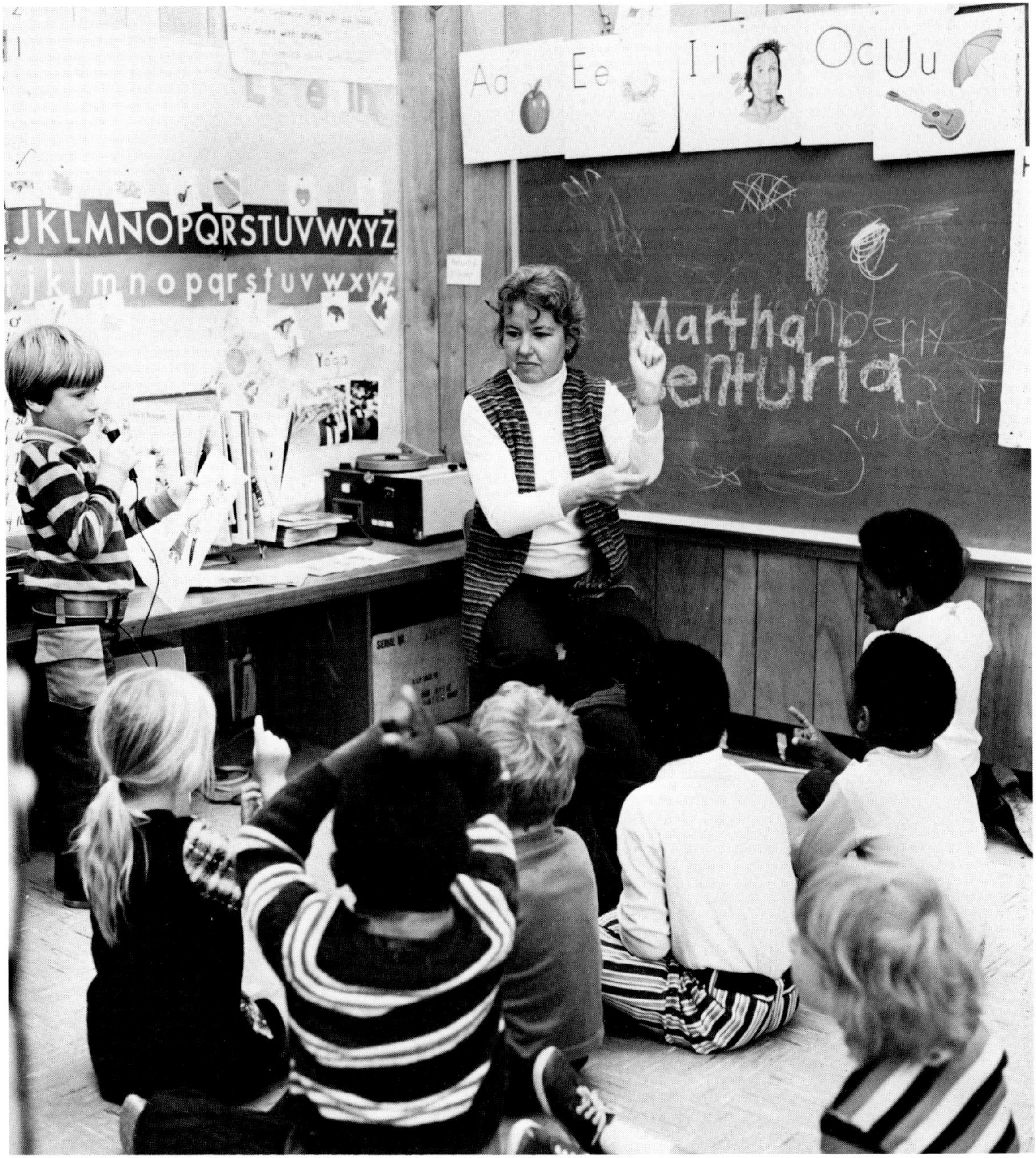
JKLMNOPQRSTUVWXYZ
Aa
Ee
Ii
Uu
Yoga
Martha

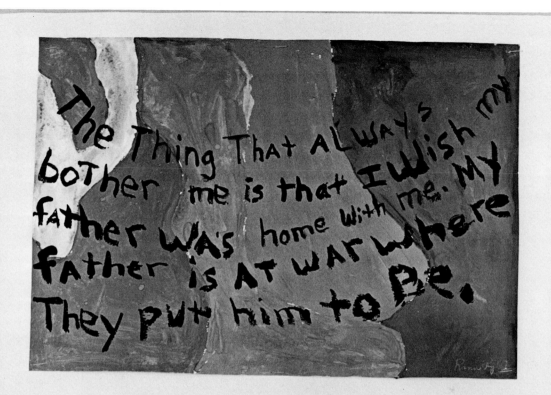

The Thing That always bother me is that I Wish my father was home with me. MY father is AT WAR where They put him to Be.

LOCAL FIRE ALARM

BREAK GLASS

"... lessons learned about
one's essential value as a person ..."

"He told me he worried about the white children
and I told him I worried about the Negro children."

"...uncertainty; tentativeness; the reaching
out that children demonstrate, whatever their
hesitations; a beginning of friendliness and trust."

CHRONICLE OF EVENTS
Leading to Desegregation in Berkeley

Winter 1957   The NAACP and a community group called the Committee on the Berkeley Schools raised the issue of school segregation in a report presented to the School Board.

Summer 1958   After six months of urging by the NAACP, the Board appointed a citizens' committee to "study certain interracial problems in the Berkeley schools and their effect on education."

Fall 1959   The committee reported on ways to improve certain aspects of the human relations climate in the schools. It did not recommend any degree of desegregation. Changes implemented as a result of the citizens' study included the creation of an Intergroup Education Office, the hiring of more minority teachers, and a reassessment of textbook content.

1962   Spokesmen for the Congress of Racial Equality charged the District with failure to meet the needs of black students, and asked the Board to appoint a committee to study the problem of de facto segregation in depth, and to recommend steps to remedy the situation.

January 1963   The Citizens' Committee on De Facto Segregation was formed of thirty-six citizens representing a cross section of the community.

November 1963 The committee reported its finding that residential segregation had created racial isolation in Berkeley's schools. Almost all of the black youth attended four schools in the lower section of the community and one of the three junior high schools. It recommended total desegregation, kindergarten through secondary school, and presented alternate plans by which this could be achieved.

Winter 1963 Public reaction to this recommendation was intense.

Spring 1964 A series of public meetings was held, heavily attended. Strong opposition to desegregation was expressed by a considerable segment of the community. Alternate desegregation plans were proposed by some citizens, and discussed.

Spring 1964 A five-member committee made up of members of the Berkeley school staff studied staff reactions to various desegregation plans. Meanwhile, every parent group in the city held a public meeting to discuss the citizens' committee findings and the various plans for desegregation.

March 1964 The Superintendent was asked by the Board to study one of the plans from the standpoint of educational goals and feasibility.

May 1964 The Superintendent recommended that the Board adopt this plan, calling for total desegregation of all grades. The Board voted unanimously to adopt that part of the plan affecting the secondary schools and to table that part dealing with the elementary schools. No District conducted busing was involved in desegregating the secondary schools, as transportation is provided by each family unit from seventh grade on.

Opponents of desegregation, forming a group called Parents for Neighborhood Schools, circulated petitions and obtained ten thousand signatures, forcing an election intended to recall the School Board. Support for the Board was organized by desegregation advocates of all races, calling themselves the Friends of the Berkeley Schools. The election was set for October 6.

Summer 1964 The debate continued through the summer. Meetings were continuous and generally highly agitated. The controversy eventually touched almost everyone in the community.

October 6, 1964 The recall move was defeated by a large plurality, indicating citizen support for the Board and its action. Implementation of the plan had begun at the opening of school the month before.

February 1966 Elementary desegregation begins. With federal funds, 240 elementary students from the four predominantly black schools were bused to schools in the hills to reduce class size in their neighborhood schools and to provide the community with the beginning of a model of interracial education.

April 1967 After hearing appeals from civil rights and teacher groups for an end to segregation in all grades, the Board unanimously agreed that it was time to bring integration to the elementary schools.

May 16, 1967   A timetable was set. Elementary desegregation was to be implemented no later than the fall of 1968. The Board committed itself to adopting a specific plan no later than January 1968, to provide time for preparation of staff, students, and community.

Summer 1967   A seven-member District task force worked through the summer examining the many community suggestions on ways to desegregate and the many plans submitted by institutes and study groups throughout the nation.

Fall 1967   At a meeting of the entire school staff, and then at a huge public meeting, five plans were presented by the task force. A series of meetings was held to elicit views of staff and community. Careful attention was placed on keeping public and school staff closely informed of all developments. Many community meetings were held, and the District sent representatives to all of them.

October 1967   The Superintendent formed a committee of thirty-five educators, and with them selected the kindergarten-three, four-six prototype for reorganization of the elementary schools. Their recommendation was announced at a mass meeting, and more community meetings ensued.

An Office of Elementary Integration was established. A Speakers' Bureau operating from this office supplied resource persons for informational meetings on the forthcoming change.

The dialogue continued through the winter, but the debate did not reach the emotional level that had characterized the previous struggle over secondary desegregation. The District directed the dialogue toward the question "How do we do it?" rather than "Should we do it?" Opposition was sporadically loud but minor. Those who did not agree were largely submitting without strong resistance.

January 1968 At a meeting attended by over two thousand people, the Board adopted the plan for desegregation of the elementary schools.

Fall 1968 The buses began to roll.

"Perhaps most of all we wonder: what will happen
to those children later on?...Will a substantial
amount of fine, sensitive schooling be the prelude
to a more decent and honorable life?...Or will
splendid early lessons later be seen as illusions...?"